"Anthologies can become a call for understanding, for tolerance, and a sense of identity. They can become a place to feel safe and secure, and to ensure the dignity of others, through connection, and noticing. That is, if we notice, we can include those differences we observe into our community, and attempt to make ourselves, individual by individual, a better and more inclusive humanity. Haiku can allow us to be a bigger part of ourselves if we allow the "little poem" to build new bridges.

If we do not notice can we have empathy, one of the most basic building blocks of "being", and of being a human? This book helps us listen between the cracks of moonlight, and pulls aside the first rays of sunlight, to find those bridges. These short poems deal with humour, and sadness, and the in-betweenness we sometimes cannot utter aloud. It encapsulates moments often deemed so irrelevant in daily life they become invisible, but they are stepping stones to our identity. Make this anthology a touchstone to construct new bridges for you."

Alan Summers
President, United Haiku and Tanka Society
co-founder, Call of the Page

"From a wildly clanging chain to chickens scratching on new snow, we are immersed in the moment with each poem. The group masterfully bridges the space between poet and reader. Sometimes somber, sometimes surprising. A fine range of insight and humor such as Johnny Baranski's one line "her rough edges smooth to a lover's touch". We can feel the love for his memory in several tribute poems including this one by Carolyn Winkler, 'watching over us / the words he left / behind'."

Sidney Bending
Haiku Arbutus

"What I enjoy most about this anthology is the love you can feel in the words for passed-on poets, and for each other as a community. It is also a fine mix of new and experienced poets with gems on each page. The diversity of styles, content, and forms shows the talent and vibrancy of The Portland Haiku Group. You can feel, while admiring the poems, prose, pictures, and dedications, that the Group pulled together to create a substantial contribution to haiku literature in the Pacific Northwest. I congratulate the editor and The Portland Haiku Group as a whole for making this heartfelt and inviting collection that I am sure local poets, and even international poets, will treasure for years to come."

Nicholas Klacsanzky

New Bridges

The Portland Haiku Group Anthology

Edited by

Jacob Salzer

& The Portland Haiku Group

2018

foreword

Throughout history, there have been poets who may have left us, but continue to inspire so that we can connect with each other, in both old and new, obvious and subtle ways. This anthology is dedicated to two such poets: Lorraine Ellis Harr who passed away more than a decade ago, still sending out ripples; and Johnny Baranski, who has only just left us, but his humor and stance for peace is a benchmark. Our loss is still very fresh, and it's wonderful to still have Johnny with us in this book. But both poets, and others who have left us recently, seem to still create and pass on new bridges, because we revisit them, and realise how even more important they were to us.

New bridges are not always easy to accomplish, and often there is great sacrifice, and compromise too, like touching our fingers to the setting sun (paraphrasing Clayton Beach). The sun is both hot, and close to disappearing at sundown, but we cannot let go, whatever the price. I sometimes feel poetry is an affliction that I can't cure, and it can be double-edged, wherein we want to keep it, but sometimes let it simply go, for some respite, when it can be unrelenting. But, new bridges do not come into being overnight, or without cost. As Lynne Jambor says, in a haiku, perhaps we are 'hoping to fix the here and now,' and that is a most potent phrase. As haiku in particular are often thought best to write in the immediate present, are we attempting to adjust something for the better, or highlight it? We are certainly trying to make new connections and communicate, in an age of instant information, though we have discovered it does not necessarily add instant knowledge. Are we staring at a lion in a dream, as Jacob Salzer touches on, or facing up to society in all its good and not so good aspects; simply delivering the truth, as we see it, in a way that might be retained? Johnny Baranski, a fighter against wrongs, says cicadas before and after Nagasaki, and I hope it's not just the insects, but humans, who will come through great catastrophes. Sometimes we are all too often sleeping in unseen labyrinths (paraphrasing Jacob Salzer) and new exits and entrances need to be created. As Nancy Norman says, in her Hemingwayesque six-word story, I'm painfully reminded that there are too many sparrows to be rescued, who have been loved and lost. If haiku and tanka can bridge the gap in its own way, and as people are turning to poetry in larger numbers, again, then I welcome this new anthology to be part of that. I feel that this anthology can warm a rainy day, or night, with cool jazz, and new bridges (paraphrasing Diana Saltoon).

As someone who writes a lot of haiku in one line, as well as the usual tercet form, I welcome the sections of different approaches to haiku, as well as including the seasons. And mentioning seasons, I don't think summer has ended, and that we have parted, as we continue to spin our webs (paraphrasing Margaret Chula). This anthology is part of that web spinning around the world, of poetry for people in great need, and for those of us more fortunate in life as well. This anthology has the beauty of sincronizadas that can be eaten any hour of the day, as appetizer, as breakfast, and even as a main course.

Alan Summers
President, United Haiku and Tanka Society
co-founder, Call of the Page

New Bridges

The Portland Haiku Group Anthology

"Once the child has learned to read alone, and can pick up a book without illustrations, he must become a creator, imagining the setting of the story, visualizing the characters, seeing facial expressions, hearing the inflection of voices. The author and the reader 'know' each other; they meet on the bridge of words."

Madeleine L'Engle, Walking on Water

In Memory of

Johnny Baranski
1948—2018

long before I came
long after I leave
blossoming pear

And

Lorraine Ellis Harr (Tombo)
1912—2006

Dragonfly—
Even if I could catch one
I wouldn't

New Bridges

The Portland Haiku Group Anthology

Edited by

Jacob Salzer

& The Portland Haiku Group

2018

ISBN-13: 978-1721042371

ISBN-10: 1721042377

New Bridges: The Portland Haiku Group Anthology

A CreateSpace Publication

Cover Design by Clayton Beach

Managing Editor: Jacob Salzer

dedication

long before I came
long after I leave
blossoming pear

Johnny Baranski, Lilliput Review #191

We chose this haiku by Johnny Baranski to celebrate his memory. He passed away unexpectedly in late January of 2018 when we were finalizing this anthology. Johnny was a core member of The Portland Haiku Group, a mentor to many of us, a prominent member of the Haiku Society of America, and a frequent contributor to many prominent journals and anthologies in the world of English-language haiku. Johnny wrote haiku and its related forms for over forty years. This charming poem of his struck us as a fitting elegy.

Johnny had a deep Catholic faith and it comes through in his poetry from time to time. He graduated from Loyola University with a degree in English Literature and quickly became involved with the Catholic pacifist resistance to the Vietnam War and nuclear proliferation, which eventually landed him in prison for non-violent actions. Imprisonment, redemption, and faith were frequent topics of his poetry, in addition to the usual subjects of haiku like the seasons and nature, but he also had a lighter, more playful side, often pushing the envelope of the haiku far into the bawdy reaches of the senryu tradition.

We will always remember and admire his humor, kindness, and dedication to the haiku form. Johnny was a genuine *haijin* and a wonderful friend. This anthology is dedicated to his memory.

The haiku below is Johnny's last poem, his *jisei*, or "death poem," written in the company of his three children during his final days.

one last breath
before dying—
plum blossom

   Johnny Baranski

In the following pages, we wrote special haiku to honor Johnny in memoriam.

convict 14302
a dragonfly zooms off
into the blue

Clayton Beach

a sudden absence—
his haiku reveals
his soul

Linda Dalal Sawaya

watching over us
the words he left
behind

Carolyn Winkler

his last breath
morning fog rises
into sunlight

Jacob Salzer

I heart your haiku
and you twitter
me a thank you

Tricia Knoll

Gold is
eternal . . .
Mary, too

David H. Rosen

death's release
now in unbounded
infinite peace

Diana Saltoon

on the reed
blue dragonfly
lands gently

Kevin Nusser

leaving the dust behind
dragonfly dances
in God's garden

Ellen Ankenbrock

migrating birds
in formation
salute the skies

Nancy Norman

a good throw
the baseball sails out of sight
my friend too

Shelley Baker-Gard

winter morning
a white dove ascends
into the clouds

Margaret Chula

the old jalopy
parked one last time
a darker gray

Jim Rodriguez

snow in the valley
late winter
reading his haiku

Jone Rush MacCulloch

crossing the stream
pine scent
on the wind

Thomas Martin

acknowledgments

Our book would not have been possible without several people. Grateful acknowledgment is made to the following people for their contributions, edits, and inspiration:

Ellen Ankenbrock
Shelley Baker-Gard
Johnny Baranski
Clayton Beach
Margaret Chula
Lynne Jambor
Tricia Knoll
Jone Rush MacCulloch
Thomas Martin
Nancy Norman
Kevin Nusser
Jim Rodriguez
David H. Rosen
Diana Saltoon
Jacob Salzer
Linda Dalal Sawaya
Michael Dylan Welch
Carolyn Winkler

Special thanks to the Friendly House in Portland, Oregon for offering free space for our haiku meetings.

contents

preface

New Bridges is the theme and title of our anthology. Traditionally, haiku revolves around community, sharing haiku, and building relationships. In turn, this relates directly to the actual writing of haiku, as we juxtapose images and discover subtle connections between humans and other forms of life.

Our anthology features three-line haiku, two-line haiku, one-line haiku, and tanka by both well-known and new haiku poets living in and around Portland, Oregon.

In a time when it seems more walls are being built around us, it is my hope that this anthology will encourage more people to build friendships and come together to create a better world for now and our future generations.

Jacob Salzer, Managing Editor

three-line haiku

Spring

spring storm
the old apple tree falls
its blooms unopened

Shelley Baker-Gard

chain clangs
on an empty flagpole
wind's ragged song

Nancy Norman

a soft breeze
through the oak tree
my neighbor's smile

Jacob Salzer

3

the woman
in the see-through blouse
blossoming cherries

Johnny Baranski

the kids
barefoot in the grass
counting poppies

Jim Rodriguez

deadheading
tiny seeds cling to me
forget-me-nots

Shelley Baker-Gard

spring wind
raked stones in the dry garden
flow without moving

Margaret Chula

leading the way
flowers in my
bicycle basket

Lynne Jambor

where do you go
butterfly
to rest your wings

Nancy Norman

retirement
the mountain cherry
still in bloom

Thomas Martin

the postman swings
a machete near the red butterfly
second jungle thoughts

Kevin Nusser

after a week away
the scent of home
crabapple blooms

Shelley Baker-Gard

second-hand leather-bound book
in spring's faint sunlight
smell of biscuits and rags

Tricia Knoll

forget me nots—
I leave them in the garden
with my memories

Margaret Chula

Mother Earth
in a green kimono
shades of spring

Carolyn Winkler

7

lost
on the forest path
moleskin and pen

Kevin Nusser

morning worry lost
into the whiteness
magnolia blooms

Shelley Baker-Gard

wild blackberries
blossoms already falling—
white butterflies

Shirley A. Plummer

Summer

sea anemones
I touch my finger to
the setting sun

Clayton Beach

on the hot tub edge
she warms her wings
damselfly

Shelley Baker-Gard

hot summer morning
on a still-shaded Buddha
drops of dew glisten

Shirley A. Plummer

9

searching for
answers from beyond—
relic radiation

Clayton Beach

stone time sunlight
the supernova
of cancer

Kevin Nusser

fingertips
tapping away the hours
oncology lobby

Clayton Beach

highlighter
hoping to fix
the here and now

Lynne Jambor

I burned a candle
hoping you'd join me
August moon

Diana Saltoon

August morning
the elderly lady settles
into her corner

Lynne Jambor

click click
of the knitting needles
grandmother

Nancy Norman

seventy-two
sunrise & sunset—
same

David H. Rosen

inside the tea hut
shadows play in dark and light
with moon and candle

Diana Saltoon

hot night
neighbor's chatter floats in
crickets too

Shelley Baker-Gard

mid-summer heat
the cleanup batter
fans three times

Johnny Baranski

summer's end
a feather rides
an updraft

Lynne Jambor

Fall

the last leaf
smacks my face
windy night

           Ellen Ankenbrock

confederate tomb
cells of the wasp nest
long empty

           Clayton Beach

prints of leaves past
on the concrete walk
dry cold day

           Shelley Baker-Gard

on this autumn shore
sea and sky meld grey to grey
void of tint or sound

Diana Saltoon

the very last thing
he couldn't hear
autumn wind

Clayton Beach

asleep
on the tatami
lines on her face

Ellen Ankenbrock

15

who am I
staring at a lion
in a dream

Jacob Salzer

joining the others
the leaves drop
one by one

Carolyn Winkler

all the leaves are brown
red dragonfly
California dreamin

Ellen Ankenbrock

dusk settles
into the rice stubble
a sickle moon

Margaret Chula

Viet Cong
haunts the rice paddies
their daughters till

Ellen Ankenbrock

cicadas before
Nagasaki
cicadas after

Johnny Baranski

17

Winter

alone at midnight
and the fire's gone out
winter rain

Margaret Chula

freezing temps
pushing the grocery cart
to the camp

Jone Rush MacCulloch

homeless man drumming
an empty beer can
winter's hard ice

Tricia Knoll

cold coffee
the sound of traffic
disappears

Lynne Jambor

icicles
words hung in the air
forgotten

Jone Rush MacCulloch

three boys and one sled
a hill
breaks the silence

Tricia Knoll

icy day
succulents stand tall
words escape

Jone Rush MacCulloch

pines sing
a long winter wind
no sleep

Ellen Ankenbrock

following
the mist, the stones
and the river

Carolyn Winkler

up and spent
between the parlor curtains
smog and moonlight

Tricia Knoll

snow geese
swaddled in clouds
winter moon

Thomas Martin

snow covered deck
textured
by tiny bird prints

Nancy Norman

alarm clock rings
while geese sound their flight
Solstice morning

Shelley Baker-Gard

winter day
throwing seeds on the deck
birds forage

Jone Rush MacCulloch

end of the walk
returning the crow's feather
where I found it

Margaret Chula

the flap of a heron
in the same direction
the plane rumbles

Shelley Baker-Gard

gray sky
the car rocks faster
over the bridge

Jim Rodriguez

Coltrane
the old jalopy
hums along

Johnny Baranski

lapping waves against iced grass
one man tunes
the foghorn

Tricia Knoll

fishing pole
the only bite
odonata

Ellen Ankenbrock

cold rains continue
this month of February
but look, plum blossoms!

Diana Saltoon

crunch of footsteps
on the rain-soaked gravel
a bullfrog croaks

Margaret Chula

the Missions
dusted with snow
a pronghorn

Jim Rodriguez

winter winds
the last low cry
of crickets

Ellen Ankenbrock

Miscellaneous

glimpsed
through a break in the clouds
starlight

Jacob Salzer

mindless chores
as red galaxies recede
into the night

Nancy Norman

loosening the nails
in the box around me
I see my shadow

Carolyn Winkler

the crowded list
of loneliness and time warps
bestsellers

Tricia Knoll

is it the sky
or just another shade
of blue

Thomas Martin

knowing
even sorrow is a dream
yet … yet …

Diana Saltoon

27

narrow path
standing on the razor's edge
is it worth it?

Ellen Ankenbrock

cell tower church steeple
the mean and meaning of war
outlives the warrior

Kevin Nusser

wrapped stone
on the garden bridge
stop

Ellen Ankenbrock

waiting for the train
so many faces hiding
stories

Diana Saltoon

glass building
inside a stranger's face
my own

Jacob Salzer

the road
to enlightenment
paved with broken mirrors

Carolyn Winkler

crow drops
crack
car crushes a walnut

Ellen Ankenbrock

the crow
hops to the car
extra fries

Jim Rodriguez

intoxicating smell
of phenol and drosophila ether
store-bought mixed drink

Kevin Nusser

this wildness
within me
a twisting vine

Carolyn Winkler

sleeping
in unseen labyrinths . . .
moles

Jacob Salzer

every morning
I walk through the dreams
of a spider

Jim Rodriguez

staring
at a familiar stranger
sunset

Jacob Salzer

bearded irises
the circus is
in town

Johnny Baranski

the little girl
twirls head over heels on
the bike rack

Jim Rodriguez

sunrise
through honeysuckle fence
roosters crow

Thomas Martin

salt water taffy
on the promenade
a bitter wind

Johnny Baranski

two-line haiku

Spring

red-breasted sapsucker
white star magnolia

David H. Rosen

counting the roses she brought
forget number again

Thomas Martin

a heron muddies clear water
opening an old love letter

Clayton Beach

crashing against the shore
waves of moonlight

Jacob Salzer

in what key
does the tide sing

Ellen Ankenbrock

gathering tsunami debris by the schoolyard
a soiled photograph

Kevin Nusser

naming spring flowers beauty
naming marine microorganisms fear

Kevin Nusser

mole tunnel labyrinths
an atom splits to pieces

Clayton Beach

how perfect this egg shell
when it's cracked

Carolyn Winkler

a rescued sparrow
loved and lost

Nancy Norman

river rocks in tall grass
the killdeer's unbroken wing

Clayton Beach

still river fading
into frogs and shadows

Thomas Martin

Summer

moonlight and cold beer . . .
summer baseball

David H. Rosen

zero sugar, zero calories
ash Wednesday

Johnny Baranski

must not be right my clicks to the junco
no reply

Shelley Baker-Gard

41

Fall

autumn sunset . . .
Grandpa's rusted license plates

Jacob Salzer

end times . . . the snake skins
we found in the barn

Thomas Martin

dense cemetery fog breaking
the silence

Jacob Salzer

Winter

so hot this field of snowflakes
Queen Anne's lace

                        Shelley Baker-Gard

all walk on water
when it is ice

                        Ellen Ankenbrock

calving icebergs
the midwifery of climate change

                        Tricia Knoll

I shake the desk when I write
wanting to shake much more

Tricia Knoll

the island of me
in a sea of history

Nancy Norman

he swims soundlessly
filling the water with peace

Nancy Norman

Miscellaneous

evening zazen
mosquitos bugging me

Johnny Baranski

packing boots, a pussy hat, and poster
March on Washington

Tricia Knoll

tiny story
snail trail

Ellen Ankenbrock

a caterpillar inside me
creating art

Carolyn Winkler

Turin international book fair
poems in unknown tongues

Kevin Nusser

the doors of consciousness
polished brass

Carolyn Winkler

Victoria's Secrets:
me, myself, and I

Johnny Baranski

inside of an iris . . .
that's where I want to be

David H. Rosen

ouch! from the falling sky
white acorns

Shelley Baker-Gard

one-line haiku

spring leaves just unfolded-first breeze

Shelley Baker-Gard

alone once more the sound of rain in f minor

Clayton Beach

empty of desire a room floods with light

Jacob Salzer

waking to crows in chorus . . . mother visits

Thomas Martin

wet knees of old jeans supplication to spring

Tricia Knoll

from a dark dank pond thirsty people drink

Kevin Nusser

bestsellers list of loneliness and time warps

Tricia Knoll

the child within still believes in magic

Nancy Norman

dusky salamanders in the spring . . . pure water

Thomas Martin

projector running . . . shadows on the wall

Carolyn Winkler

time passes . . . through Grandmother's eyes

Carolyn Winkler

worn stone a lone ant traces the lemniscate

Clayton Beach

from behind bars the moon pale faced too

Johnny Baranski

July 4th plastic ice sickles still burn

Thomas Martin

into the night the owl cries – farewell to me?

Shelley Baker-Gard

nymph alighted the lotus waiting for dry wings

Ellen Ankenbrock

her rough edges smooth to a lover's touch

Johnny Baranski

There, here, everywhere . . . Charlottesville

David H. Rosen

inside the Kamakura Buddha sitting silent

Kevin Nusser

rows of solar panels on high stanchions how people get out of the sun

Tricia Knoll

developing photo graphic memory

Jacob Salzer

the wind makes its tracks on sand

Diana Saltoon

figs oozing nectar: edible sunshine

Linda Dalal Sawaya

beware the windshield wiper cat tail

Nancy Norman

fishing after dark river sounds never fading

Jacob Salzer

orange moon apocalypses

Linda Dalal Sawaya

fireworks on my computer screen . . . the silence

Thomas Martin

his chainsaw snores butcher sleep

Nancy Norman

sirens far out my burning bridges

Johnny Baranski

my love's lilies in full bloom scorch in the sun as he dies

Linda Dalal Sawaya

water running downhill people avoid the calm

Kevin Nusser

Holding a deep red blossom . . . Heather Heyer

David H. Rosen

between I Thou the windstorm's anarchy

Johnny Baranski

mauve pillows part Venus and the moon

Shelley Baker-Gard

dark sky murmurs the surf replies in foxfire

Clayton Beach

barefoot violinist plays under a full moon

Nancy Norman

swollen river the empty vodka bottle

Jim Rodriguez

orange of autumn on cloudless blue

Shelley Baker-Gard

breathing paint filling a shadow

Jim Rodriguez

warming this rainy night shot of cool jazz

Diana Saltoon

family gathering fog between mountains

Jacob Salzer

fallen fir unconcerned warmth from his fire

Kevin Nusser

70 years of broken parts somehow glued together

Carolyn Winkler

leg-long icicle pulls at the ennui of the snowbound

Tricia Knoll

noonday sun hanging low in the sky she tells it slant

Clayton Beach

screech owl climbing into darkness

Jim Rodriguez

flowering kale for an empty heart

David H. Rosen

out of the darkest winter plum blossoms

Carolyn Winkler

tanka

the gentle curve
of a fawn's spine
in tall grass—
how many springs
have we slept through?

Clayton Beach

moving Mother
into assisted living
on April Fool's Day
I say good-bye
to her battered golf clubs

Margaret Chula

blinding dawn
in the windshield
four crows
hop the white line
near a dead squirrel

Tricia Knoll

spring flowers rising
from a dirty squirt bottle
inspired nature
living and
its trash

Kevin Nusser

Mother Earth
covered in
heavenly rain drops
she dances her hoop
in the center of the circle

Carolyn Winkler

first dogwood
blossoms slipping inside
outside twilight
your muffled gasp
as our children sleep nearby

Clayton Beach

hummingbird
quick glimpse
and gone
all the girls I loved or lost
flash through my mind

Thomas Martin

fresh halibut
closed please call again
help wanted
due to the power outage
celebrate spring

Kevin Nusser

the surf
drowned out by softness
of his words
tearful expressions talking
about his father

Jim Rodriguez

silver falls
my face dripping water
as a brown snail
slides along the wet rail
leaving a silvery track

Thomas Martin

the sign bans life—
no camping or alcohol
no littering or fires
no illegal substances . . .
Springwater Corridor trail

Kevin Nusser

a dampness
after carpet cleaning
lonely empty
rooms wondering
why bring things back

Tricia Knoll

sun on the pond
above the golden koi
children's laughter
he was here once with me
my son's voice so far away

Shelley Baker-Gard

what is truth
to a butterfly
sipping
the sweet honey centers
of white clover

Margaret Chula

70th birthday
all about the wish
not the presents
she blows out
the candles

Carolyn Winkler

Mother's Day
a long line of visitors
at the county jail
so many smiles
too many tears

Johnny Baranski

two hawks circle
scree-screaming the rabbits' run
my place at the listening post
in the shivering wind
of canyons

Tricia Knoll

a squirrel
scampers across a tight wire
and shakes
this rainy day
awake

Thomas Martin

found digging through tossed books
poems from prison
an old friend's chapbook
from 1979
protesting crimes

Kevin Nusser

in full bloom
on her wedding day
is this the girl
whose diapers
I once changed?

Johnny Baranski

the kids
barefoot in the grass
counting poppies
the things
I didn't get to do

Jim Rodriguez

muffled
behind glass
the untold stories
in my Grandma's
eyes

Jacob Salzer

hidden
on the back shelf
a small box
from her teenage years
filled with sea glass

Carolyn Winkler

clouds drift
into factory smoke
above
the Columbia River
she leaves a trail of stars

Jacob Salzer

O moon,
even on this clear night
the earth's shadow
cannot hide
your brilliance

Diana Saltoon

of all
the gin joints in the world
you sneak
into this love poem
to remind me of my loss

Thomas Martin

somewhere
within the chambers
of my heart
the voice
of my mother

Jacob Salzer

lying down
next to him every night
he asks me
for the same lullaby
please be kind

Clayton Beach

flickering above
the pond we stroll around
a circle of fireflies
you tell me they're reflections
of electric lights

Margaret Chula

he spends
every dime he earns on
the sexy Cougar
that caught his eye
at the hot rod swap meet

Johnny Baranski

Summer snow
Queen Anne's lace
waves to all
sweet pea and chicory too
my three sisters

Shelley Baker-Gard

black bird
flies into the house
a death omen?
by all means
set the bird free

Ellen Ankenbrock

peace lantern
in a world of turmoil
I wonder why
the gardener has hidden it
among the shrubs

Johnny Baranski

a single
black cloud clings
to the timberline
& yet you tell me
there's nothing wrong

Clayton Beach

rereading
a month's worth of poems
smiling, crying
you come to me
and hold my hand

Margaret Chula

absent
preferred the alcohol
and bar friends
memories
on father's day

Carolyn Winkler

all afternoon
the blue jay calls
flies off and lands again
pushing his lifeless mate
through the dry grass

Thomas Martin

lust is pasting over pain
hiding propagation
a clown face death mask
recite the same poem
sing the same song

Kevin Nusser

amazing how
we put one foot in front
of the other
and write
with a pen

Carolyn Winkler

the weight
of father's empty luggage
in my old bedroom
receipts from China drift
in the wind

Jacob Salzer

if only I had
kept it
the lottery ticket
on which I jotted
the winning haiku

Johnny Baranski

one band-tailed pigeon
blends into another
dusty trudge of poets
to the workshop
no form, no lines

Tricia Knoll

stained glass windows
from my childhood church
in storage
another reason
not to go home

Thomas Martin

elderly reimagine the past
in a theater
outside
a disturbance . . .
cops with shotguns

Kevin Nusser

unseen
behind the smile
scars
twisting what is good
and healthy in her

Jim Rodriguez

the wilted rose dies
nothing tragic
in comedic timing
leaping
conclusions

Kevin Nusser

baby
in a cradle board
corn to grind
will she remember the stone
on her journey from home?

Shelley Baker-Gard

summer has ended
and we have parted
yet spiders continue
to spin their webs from
one dead stem to another

Margaret Chula

since you left
even the moon is halved
its fullness hiding
in my heart
this dark, cold night

Diana Saltoon

before I leave
I wrap you in a warm blanket
with my bare hands and whisper:
let go of all desire
sleep without fear this night

Jacob Salzer

wet hair
dripping on my nipples
the waves
of warbling birds
and scolding crows

Tricia Knoll

displayed in the window
of a consignment shop
my old evening gown
on a flaxen-haired manikin
the size I once was

Margaret Chula

vague shadows
the spruce hidden
in dense fog
what was it you wrote
in your diary today?

Clayton Beach

when you didn't return
I gave the flowers to
a woman
on the railway platform
who looks just like you

Johnny Baranski

naturally revealed—
the clear moon and stars
in the stillness
of the lake
in my heart

Diana Saltoon

the raindrops
gather salt on
their journey
down my nose
yes—I licked them

Shelley Baker-Gard

92

cool nights arrive
not much hope left—
for red tomatoes
now in my autumn years I
cherry-pick a lot more

Shelley Baker-Gard

maple leaves
swirling
in puddles . . .
dancing
dervishes

Ellen Ankenbrock

in your absence
the full moon
the milky way
the emptiness
they cannot satisfy

Johnny Baranski

cloud tufts
caught on the tips
of the fir trees
the scent of your hair
still clings to my pillow

Clayton Beach

you left—
and the rains began
steady as the tears
forming rivers
down my dress

Diana Saltoon

walking alone
why do I keep looking
at the moon?
the cold night fills
with unheard voices

Jacob Salzer

windows to old days
absent of eyes or ears
the blood
in the veins of my hands
boil in a dream

Tricia Knoll

I awake at dusk
from a feverish slumber
a day gone by and
the last leaves have fallen
from the copper beach

Margaret Chula

all these years
still punishing
their Mother
for the Stepfather's
broken sticks

Carolyn Winkler

like that wooden bench
in your garden
on which we first kissed
you and I
have seen better days

Johnny Baranski

waves
ceaselessly crash
against the shore
I walk beside you
without a sound

Jacob Salzer

your hand held dearly
melts away
in this rain—
are these withered bones
mine or yours?

Diana Saltoon

stoically
grandmother stands
in front of her painting
photo at
the funeral

Carolyn Winkler

pausing
on the tracks
I look for movement
the slow rise and fall
of his belly

Jacob Salzer

the red glow
of the winter sunset
in the bare trees
empty bird nests appear
in the cold, clear air

Thomas Martin

forecast of snow flurries
on withered beets
through morning fog
the memories
of her breast cancer

Tricia Knoll

estranged father
writes that he loves me
misspells my name
outside the window
chickens scratch on new snow

Margaret Chula

3 am, my breath
the edge of our galaxy
winter glistening
a hint of your perfume
still lingers on my shirt

Clayton Beach

closed
this deserted carnival
for winter
in a small tidal pool
a moon jelly in moonlight

Thomas Martin

surrounded by night
the man stares
into the fire
does he see a lost home?
his tent door opens

Shelley Baker-Gard

he sits on my lap
this wiry husband
explaining his late hours
I cannot see
snow falling

Tricia Knoll

where does
this consciousness reside
after death
the atoms still
spinning

Carolyn Winkler

stripped Jeep
the rusty chassis engulfed
in brambles
a ruby crowned kinglet
darts through the window

Clayton Beach

publication credits

Some haiku and tanka in this anthology have received awards and honorable mentions listed below. In addition, many haiku and tanka appear in the following journals, books, and anthologies:

Journals

A Hundred Gourds
American Tanka
Atlas Poetica
Bones
Bottle Rockets
Cattails
Chrysanthemum
Kernels
Frogpond
Haibun Today
Haiku Canada Review
Lilliput Review
Modern Haiku
Otata
Prune Juice
Ribbons
Skylark
The Heron's Nest
Tinywords
Under the Basho
Wild Plum

Awards and Honorable Mentions

Harold Henderson Haiku Contest, first honorable mention, 2010 ("end of the walk" by Margaret Chula)

Itoen Tea Haiku Contest winner, 2009 ("dusk settles" by Margaret Chula)

The Second Mainichi Haiku Contest, second prize, 1998 ("spring wind" by Margaret Chula)

A *zatsuei* (haiku of merit) award, *World Haiku Review* 2012; Plumtree Press, booklet for Northwest Concord 2014 presenters, seven poems from the Advisory Board ("wild blackberries" by Shirley A. Plummer)

Books and Anthologies

Always Filling, Always Full, White Pine Press, 2001
Just This, Mountains & Rivers Press, 2013
This Moment, Katsura Press, 1995
On Down the Road: 2017 Haiku Society of America Members Anthology, 2017
Tuesday Anthology, 2014
Fog Between Mountains, CreateSpace, 2018

bios

Ellen Ankenbrock was born in the year of the dragon and currently living a charmed life surrounded by wonderful, kind, and talented people and animals helping her pursue the muses. She knows things.

Shelley Baker-Gard was born in Portland, Oregon, and still walks its streets. She earned a BS degree in Anthropology and a MS in Communications. She first became interested in haiku at Cleveland high school and then put it aside for several decades. About six years ago, she began writing haiku inspired by beautiful moments during her daily bike commute to work along a nature trial. For the past three years, she has served as the Haiku Society of America regional coordinator for Oregon and has haiku published in anthologies. Her favorite classical haiku poet is Kobayashi Issa because he talked to frogs, too.

Johnny Baranski (1948—2018) published his first haiku in 1975. Since then his haiku and its related forms have appeared in numerous publications and anthologies. He is the author of several chapbooks: *Silent Silos*: A CounterBOMB Haiku Sequence, *Fish Pond Moon, Hitch Haiku, Pencil Flowers: Jail Haiku, Convicts Shoot the Breeze,* and *Blossoming Pear.* He also co-wrote a new haiku book: *White Rose, Red Rose* with David H. Rosen. His latest collection *Fireweed* has been accepted for publication by Folded Word Press.

Clayton Beach has been writing poetry since 1999. Finding inspiration in music, the sciences, philosophy and the natural world, his writing is syncretic and draws deeply from Western as well as Eastern traditions. His work has appeared in a variety of literary journals including *Frogpond, Acorn, The Heron's Nest, Bottle Rockets, Otata, and American Tanka*. He enjoys hunting wild mushrooms, growing bonsai and succulents, playing classical piano and dancing Argentine tango. He lives in Portland, Oregon with his wife and two children.

Margaret Chula began writing haiku and tanka in 1980 while living in Kyoto, Japan. She has been a featured speaker and workshop leader at writers' conferences throughout the U.S. as well as Poland, Canada, and Japan. Her eight collections of poetry include *Grinding my ink*, which won the Haiku Society of America Book Award. Maggie served for five years as president of the Tanka Society of America. Her haiku, tanka, and haibun explore the interconnection between our everyday lives and the natural world—observations that are often amusing, occasionally profound.

Lynne Jambor regards herself as "a grasshopper in the haiku world." She currently lives in Vancouver, BC between ocean and mountain.

Tricia Knoll is a Portland poet who maintains a daily haiku practice. Her collected poems include *Urban Wild* (Finishing Line Press), *Ocean's Laughter* (Aldrich Press) and *Broadfork Farm* (The Poetry Box.) Her book of poetry *How I Learned to Be White* will be out from Antrim House in 2018. Her website is: triciaknoll.com

Jone Rush MacCulloch is a teacher-librarian during the school year, and a blogger, poet, and writer the rest of the time. She shares her poetry passion with students through a club, Poetry Rocks: Performance Poetry and her annual Poetry Postcard Project is now in its tenth year. Jone is published in *The Poetry Friday Anthology for Celebrations* by Sylvia Vardell and Janet Wong, *The Best of Today's Little Ditty*: 2014—2015 (Volume 1), and *The Best of Today's Little Ditty*: 2016 (Volume 2) by Michelle Heidenrich Barnes. Outside of school and writing, she likes taking road trips with her husband and her dachshund, Buster, and hanging out with family. She usually has a camera, pen, and notebook in hand. Find her online at https://deowriter.wordpress.com/ and on twitter @JoneMac53.

Thomas Martin was born on a farm, but lives with his talented spouse, Joyce, in the Pacific Northwest of the USA. He has haiku, tanka, and haibun published in many journals both in print and online. He is a graduate of the University of North Carolina at Chapel Hill and has published three books: *Real Gifts*, *A Southern Line*, and *Where the Light Falls*. He has won numerous awards for his poetry, including the appearance of one of his haiku on the cover of *Mayfly*. He is currently working on collections of tanka and haibun.

Nancy Norman is primarily a painter. She has won many awards for her work, locally, statewide, and internationally. She began writing poetry many years ago. She joined the Portland Haiku Group in the past year. "Now I find myself writing haiku in my mind while observing life around me, creating a peaceful Awareness. I think of my paintings as poetry."

Kevin Nusser is an adherent and opponent of nihilism fighting to find meaning in a mean world. He has been writing poems, short stories, and words for the past fifty years with his first poem published at six years old in "A Letter to Grandma." He is suspicious of sincerity and conviction, but a firm believer in challenge over happiness. He is published in the *Chinese Journal of Physiology, Prostaglandins, Endocrine, Human Reproduction, Biology of Reproduction* and *Advanced Experimental Medical Biology*. He has degrees in Microbiology, Animal Science, Education, Statistics and Reproductive Biology. While his writing goals as a poet is to die unpublished, his poems have appeared in online blogs, anthologies and websites. He lives in Portland, Oregon.

Jim Rodriguez has been writing haiku since he was first introduced to the art form when he was in the fifth grade, and couldn't grasp a poem that didn't rhyme. He has since become a member of HSA and is active with the Portland Haiku Group and Haiku Northwest up in Seattle, Washington. He has been published in *World Haiku* several times, *Frogpond, The Heron's Nest*, and most of the *Seabeck Haiku Anthology* issues.

David H. Rosen was born in Port Chester, New York in 1945. He currently lives in Eugene, Oregon. David is a physician & Jungian analyst, and the author of fifteen books including: *Transforming Depression: Healing the Soul Through Creativity*, *The Tao of Jung: The Way of Integrity*, *Lost in the Long White Cloud: Finding My Way Home*, *The Tao of Elvis*, and several collections of haiku and little poems including: *The Healing Spirit of Haiku* with Joel Weishaus; *Spelunking Through Life*; *Living with Evergreens*; and *In Search of the Hidden Pond*. Forthcoming is forty years of verse Torii Haiku: *Profane to the Sacred*. In 2017, Oxford University Press published *Patient-Centered Medicine: A Human Experience* by David Rosen and Uyen Hoang.

Diana Saltoon was introduced to *chado*, the way of tea, at the Green Gulch Zen Center near San Francisco, California. She received a certificate of Chamei from the Urasenke School in Kyoto, Japan, and was a teacher at the Portland Wakai Tea Association in Oregon before moving to New York in 2011. In 2014, she returned to Portland, Oregon, where she now resides. A member of Zen communities in Oregon and New York, Diana gives presentations, classes and workshops on the Zen art of tea. She is also a member of the Portland Haiku Group, the author of *Wife, Just Let Go: Zen, Alzheimer's, and Love*, with Robert Briggs (2017), *Tea and Ceremony* (2004), *The Common Book of Consciousness* (1990), and *Four Hands: Green Gulch Poems* (1987). Her website is: dianasaltoon.blogspot.com

Jacob Salzer has been writing haiku since 2006. His haiku, tanka, and haibun are published in *Frogpond, Modern Haiku, Under the Basho, Chrysanthemum, A Hundred Gourds, Atlas Poetica, Haiku Canada Review, Prune Juice,* and *The Heron's Nest*. In 2016, he served as the managing editor for the Haiku Nook Google+ anthology: *Yanty's Butterfly*. He is currently managing another *Haiku Nook Google+ anthology* dedicated to the 600+ million people who don't have access to clean water. He is also active in the Portland Haiku Group in Portland, Oregon. He lives in the Pacific Northwest, USA. The website for Yanty's Butterfly: Haiku Nook G+ Anthology can be found at: https://jsalzer.wixsite.com/yantysbutterfly

Linda Dalal Sawaya is a Lebanese American artist and writer. Her book, *Alice's Kitchen: Traditional Lebanese Cooking*, has authentic immigrant recipes sprinkled with a generous amount of memoir. She was introduced to haiku in a 2002 retreat in the Arizona desert with Angeles Arrien, whose delightful assignment was to write one haiku every day for the ten-day retreat to be shared aloud with the group. The skillful Portland Haiku group rekindled her fondness for this form of expression, and has expanded her knowledge about its contemporary parameters in the instructional monthly meetings.

Her websites are:

lindasawaya.com
aliceskitchencookbook.com

Carolyn Winkler lives in Portland and, along with Shelley Baker-Gard, began the current Portland Haiku Group in October, 2014. They wanted to give people interested in haiku a place to come together, share, and learn. Carolyn was introduced to haiku through her study of *Chanoyu*, Japanese Way of Tea. She began writing them in 2012 and, for her, it has become a spiritual practice, connecting her inner and outer worlds. She also creates and teaches Personal Growth Workshops and Study Groups to help people discover their authentic selves and create better lives. Her Intuitive Painting Workshops motto is "Just follow the paint, it takes you where you need to go." For her, reading and writing haiku, does the same.

Her website is:

http://spiritmaskjourneys.com/

about us

The Portland Haiku Group in Portland, Oregon was founded by Shelley Baker-Gard and Carolyn Winkler. The mission of the Portland Haiku Group is to provide respectful, fun, face-to-face meetings where we can come together to share our haiku and support each other in the further development and appreciation of this poetry form originating from Japanese culture.

For more information, including links to online haiku and tanka journals, please visit our Portland Haiku Group website:

https://jsalzer.wixsite.com/portlandhaikugroup

index

Jim Lewis ... Intro Photo: "Cascade Springs";
36(p) "Red Bridge"

Thomas Martin ... *xiii*, 6, 21, 27, 33, 37, 40, 42, 51,
52, 53, 56, 64(p), 68, 69, 73, 77, 83, 86, 100, 102,
112

Nancy Norman ... *xii*, 3, 5, 12, 21, 26, 40, 44, 52,
55, 56, 58, 112

Kevin Nusser ... *xii*, 6, 8, 10, 28, 30, 38, 39, 46,
48(p), 52, 54, 57, 59, 66, 68, 70, 74, 83, 86, 87, 113

Jim Rodriguez ... *x*(p), *xiii*, *xvi*(p), 4, 23, 25, 30, 31,
32, 34(p), 58, 60, 69, 75, 87, 113

David H. Rosen ... *xii*, 12, 37, 41, 47, 54, 57, 60,
109

Diana Saltoon ... *xii*, *xx*(p), 11, 12, 15, 24, 27, 29,
55, 58, 77, 89, 92, 95, 98, 114

Jacob Salzer ... *xi*, 3, 16, 26, 29, 31, 32, 38, 42, 51,
55, 59, 75, 76, 78, 84, 89, 95, 98, 99, 115

Linda Dalal Sawaya ... *xi*, 2(p), 55, 56, 115

Carolyn Winkler ... *xi*, *xviii*(p), 7, 16, 20, 26, 29,
31, 39, 46, 52, 53, 59, 60, 67, 72, 76, 82, 84, 97, 99,
103, 116

Made in the USA
San Bernardino, CA
16 July 2018